The Overlay
of Random
and Order

The Overlay
of Random
and Order

Selected Poems

Jan Dunbar

The poet and publisher express their appreciation to the following publications in which some of these poems first appeared: *Gray's Sporting Journal* ("The Angled One," "Juliana"), *Plainswoman* ("The Bull," "The Old Lady and the Ravens"), *Yokoi* ("Autumn Day," "Long Distance," "Turncoat," "Upstairs"). "The Gatherers" appeared in *The Huckleberry Book* (American Geographic, 1988); "Montana Aurora" appeared in *Aurora* (Bull Thistle Press, 1991); "The Bull" was reprinted in *Montana Sketchbook* (Montana Institute of the Arts, 1989).

Set in 11-point Baskerville, the typeface designed by the eighteenth-century English printer and artist John Baskerville, this book is printed on Springhill opaque vellum, an acid-free stock.

Cover and division pages: Details from *Ephemera,* a woodcut by Dustin Dunbar

Printed in the United States of America
Text and cover design by Write Stuff Communications

Library of Congress Catalog Card Number: 97-67160
ISBN: 1-889087-02-5

P.S., A PRESS
169 Garron Road
Middletown Springs, VT 05757
Phone/fax: 802-235-2844

For Cal, of course

Contents

Juliana   1

The Angled One   5
Trappings   7
The Gatherers   9
An Anniversary Poem   11
Conglomerate   13
Three-Day Business Trip: A Love Poem   14
Ridinghood   16
The Clock   17
Long Weekend   18
Passages   20

Montana Aurora   23
The Old Lady and the Ravens   24
Bay by Bird Island   26
The Walk   28
A New Old Sky   30
Closing the Cabin   31
The Woodrat   32
Dragonfly   34
The Raven   35

Below the Wasatch Front   39
Itinerant Photographer at the Ranch, 1883   41
Old Wife's Tale   43
After the Auction   44
Indian Summer   45
Ritual   47

Tea with Grandmother Horlick   49
CCC, 1933   51
The Biggest Man in the World   53
The Bull   55
Impromptu Dump   57

The Widow   61
The Mallard   63
Full Circle   64
The Harvest   65
The Bivalves: Widow's Bric-a-Brac   66
Autumn Day   68
Robin Hood   69
Divestiture   71
Slipping at the Opera   72
Long Distance   74
Subterfuges   75
At St. Joseph's   76
Geraniums   77
In the Absence of a Will   78
The Letters   79
The Other Side   80

The Antisocial Norm   83
Art Show   85
Easter Snow   86
Anasazi Rain   87
The Road under My House   88
Eight A.M.   89
Upstairs   90
Pending   91
Real Estate at Portal Creek   92
After the Walk   93

Horse Butte   94
Fire Danger   95
The Firehole   96

Meteor Shower   99
Phaeton   100
The New Pump   101
Walking Her Man   102
There Went the Bride   103
Motel in Missoula   104
American Legion Convenes at Big Timber   106
Off-Season   107
Turncoat   109
It Is Spring–Somewhere   110
Cattle Drive up the Madison   111
High Places   112
At the Charles M. Russell Gallery   114
Message from a Deserted Cabin   115

Juliana

St. Albans, 1450

Often in the way of the novice,
Juliana prayed with her eyes open,
open eyes like Chaucer's *fowles.*
It was Merry England, green
through all the night,
though the king murdered
and the plague made simple the wise.

In leaping times when
up and out of the glittering stones
through the bubbles and mosses
came the mayflies in speckles and silks,
plumed like herself in nun's wimple,
skating the slick of the surface,
the ice of summer, dancing creation
in quadrilles and gavottes, snagging
Juliana's prayer, netting her glance,

she, the emerger, not knowing her place,
innocent of prerogatives reserved for God,
sensed the sublime of the miniature world,
the drippy secrets of silver and weeds,
the overlay of random and order,
seduction of lures, beguiling as His
to catch as if frog-tongues the slippery ones,
where *ye trought lepyth.*

It was too good to keep.
She invaded creation with a key,
setting sail her secular parchment,
her keys to the secrets of the weeds—

the way of the *fysshe* with the fly,
the way of the silk and the *hoke*,
the filtered glance through the willow,
the shadow's fall, like the sparrow's,
in league with the heavens—she,
treading guileless across the man's world,
though the king murdered
and the plague made simple the wise.

The Angled One

You call late, padding the snag of your excuse,
the fish of your mind still parting the water,
caught yet by the fly you present so daintily,
imitating ephemeridae.

You are breathless, sweaty in the damp booth,
snagged by the need to tell and to revel.
Your voice sounds as Neptune might in the sea cave,
mystic and wet.

The trout rose to you and you were amazed,
standing in the rain as if the hours
were stitched still by clouds,
amazed that today he did the predictable,
could not resist you,
could not drown the suspicion that this one,
dubbed fur and deer hair, was not
the wing of the exquisite truth.
Five pounds at least allowed you to play against
the tug of his angularity,
the genius of his movement,
the career of escape into the nebula of the weedbeds.

Trout, left behind when his slimy cousins
climbed out of the seas,
swims in the lake as he always has,
silver and quick, staring you down endlessly
through his clever, blinkless defiance.

He bent your hook, tore loose and flashed away,
flipping once through his own foamy slice,
down, down into the green silence of his victory.

He works in your memory as the proverbial,
the phantom of your daydreams,
the totem of your desire,
the elusive adversary of your ego,
and you love him best now,
smug in his weedbed.
For he is, as you are,
what imagination begets.

Trappings

Seven a.m.,
life follows art in the Winslow Homer of it,
the hat with flaps, the drabness of vest,
the measles of tiny flies stuck upon it
with unnatural regularity, pretending hatch;
studied camouflage, the tiger hidden in lush jungle,
except for the glitter of your eyes.

Brittle in a miracle of bending,
the rod rests, the dueling rapier with its own touché.
Little boxes full of little boxes
bounce in a sack, bits of exotic fluff
hiding the barbless hooks of fair play;
extra leaders stashed, a pendulum of scissors
swinging, field glasses making an unnatural bulge,
lunch crushed underarm, thermos sloshing,
and the net, always the sign of hope.

All float in the boat's damp puddle
from yesterday's shower.
The rod, for all its standing as Most Prized Possession,
teeters over the oars.
The vest will save your life, I'm told,
though you'll take it off in the heat of ten o'clock.
For now the latent monster of a lake rests,
reflecting its own violence in the mirror
of its momentary neutrality.
Your motored craft, silver as a knife,
cuts its wound across the surface,
put-putting a triangle in its stealth across the slick,
the emperor's new clothes of deceit.
A lie says browns are looking the other way.

You will cast against such a lapse,
the one weak moment when the cruising alter ego
will sip the hackled hook, joining for a moment
his unlikely instinct to your own.

The Gatherers

The word gets out like Sutter's mill.
They're on! It's happening, like gold in the sluicebox,
the huckleberries are ripe. Now.
I can smell them.

    The ritual of the gatherers.
    The lard buckets.
    The grandmothers.
    The great-grandmothers.

It is at dawn we go, the daughter and I.
Thirty miles away at sixty miles an hour.
I can smell them.

    He thinks we're crazy
    as he ties the leader to the line
    here on the dry river of his study.
    A good knot. Might hold a three-pounder.

Crazy, yes. Mosquitoes, horseflies, ants,
bears–and what do you have?
A stiff back, purple fingers,
minuscule berries for skimpy pies.
So why do we do it?

    His eyes ask without looking up
    from his fly box.
    He's right, and we know it.
    I don't know why we go.

Later, deep in the knee joint, there's a message:

Our mother did it.
Our grandmother did it.
They and their mothers gathered and knelt,
pushing aside crinkled leaves for these small treasures
since forever, and before that.
We go too. We do this now.

It's like fishing, I tell him,
but I see he doesn't understand.
The trout he puts back to catch again,
but the pie he'll only eat.

An Anniversary Poem

He eats his dinner, a dutiful participant,
eyes on the *New York Times*
while the chicken breasts in cognac
turn rubbery in their mushrooms.
Carrot sticks swim like worms.
Outside a mountain bluebird blinks in the hose spray,
two cats eyeing him across the boundaries, waiting.
Dusk tries to sweat rain.
Another blue cloud turns left and skips the town.
She waits, flushed by the skip
between micro and stove, panting in hopes
of a *Good Housekeeping* Seal of Approval.
It should be enough that he swallows, content.
But it is not.

Mathematically, it is dinner number 12,150,
better than the first 500,
but expertise plateaus in habit,
doomed like an eel in the filter.

She calls him back.
        Like it.
        Please like it.
        Like it, dammit!

He leaves her scrutiny, finding solace in the bathroom
for the hausfrau she has become.
She goes out to move the hoses, wondering
where the magic turned left with the clouds.
Tomorrow she'll try shrimp.

Perhaps she should sell the house.
Perhaps she will give it to him,

letting someone else worry the windows.
Perhaps he will rent a condo, no birds, no hoses,
where he will go secretly with the brown-thighed girl
with the swinging hips who does aerobics.

Perhaps it will rain
and he will get news in the mail
that an unknown uncle has died and left him millions.
It will all be in the *New York Times*.

Conglomerate

There are notes all over the mirror,
yellow Post-its at random,
helter-skelter to attract your attention,
things like:
    Funeral, either 12 or 1, Friday . . . and
        Pick up Bromfield . . . and
            Your motor is ready.
These are the business of our lives.
These are the graffiti of the bathroom,
the room where I know you will not miss seeing the notes,
the room where the mirror shows you again who you are,
the wider forehead and the bristles of white hair,
the room where what I do shows on the mirror.

My life is separated and sorted by stick-ons,
and not one of them says I love you,
only that I answer the phone when it rings
in the way of being present.

Three-Day Business Trip: A Love Poem

American women must learn to be widows.
—A probate officer

It is a special way of being alone,
a trial run as if computers simulated
a Three Mile Island sort of disaster.
For me, a meltdown of you.
All the red lights scream.
It is the end.
You are gone.
The trial means I pretend.
How would it be?
I have the house, the yard,
and time, my own time to myself.
My own trials, too,
the garbage of my day
to sort through alone.
How would I be?

I lock the door, and then I listen.
I listen for the tread of alien footsteps.
I see the birds, the wind.
I must practice a day without you as my focus.
I stop saving details for discussion.
I must empty my own mousetraps,
throw my own splatters
of feathers against the windows
to the cats for cleanup.

I sense the exhilaration of no accounting.
The need to be or to do this or that is gone.

I can relax into the drunkenness of nonduty,
a euphoria of no shirts, no socks, no mud.
I feel the excitement of time alone,
just mine.

I know it would last a week or so,
and then I would Faust my soul to the devil
to get you back again.
Thank you, but the performance will be ad lib.
It will be probate from scratch.

Ridinghood

It is my idea to send her
alone, if need be, to pick up the old lady.
Somebody has to go. Why should it always be me?

She takes apples and an afghan,
tanks up, having chosen the bad car
because, oh, because it has a tape deck.

The five-hour drive takes two days—one way.
Blizzard. Whiteout. Frosted throttle.
Of course there would be a frosted throttle.

Now I wait. I braise beef and onions
and count the minutes.
The wind whirls snow at the window
and makes a stew of me.
I'll laugh when they burst in, special delivery,
the old and the young. I'll warm them
and whoop at their bravery.

If they don't come? If it snows all night?
Hostage, I peel potatoes in silence.

The Clock

Long ago the boy buried his alarm clock
under the window-tree. He would not say why.
Fathers are good at narrowing
to that one best intelligent thing to do:
the intelligent thing to do was nothing.

Mothers do not narrow well,
especially concerning alarm clocks.
They like a Chinese guessing game
only when all the shells hold peas.
Now the boy must go.

Stiff-lipped, we arm him with bold ties,
a charge card, and a brand new alarm clock.
We are good and right and sensible.

We do not cry. We look at the earth
while it lurches in its orbit.
We are dry lumps being swallowed.

But when I walk beside the window-tree,
I hear the old clock ticking up the grass
and marvel that time dares go backwards,
recklessly, from so far underground.

Long Weekend

The vacuum cleaner has purred and done its miracle;
the dryer has bumped, fluffed, bounced
its lyrical homage to renewal;
ravages wrought upon the mirrors
have been polished twice.
The savages have taken the skis, jackets,
sleeping bags, and, warily, the packets
of leftover roast, sandwiches,
thermoses, Milky Ways, and cans
of things I never meant to give away,
leaving the shelves like scorched earth.

They've gone. "The locusts," we say in jest,
gone like hocus-pocus after a flight of noise
and giggling exuberance. They infested the air
with bangs to the doors and strange rites of music,
a knock of sound for every hour.
    "How very, oh, how wonderful
      that Dad can work the stereo."

How quaint we are, but pleasant.
Pretty game–for old folks.

    But all the same, it would be nice
    if they had forgotten something.
    Contacts, perhaps, or the dark boy's guitar,
    drawing them back, bringing this silence
    to a kind of life.

I am not ready to give them up again,
to do this bit of homage to the Great Pizza Parlor in the Sky.

I anger at my own campaign to gear them up to flight,
to cast us off like old diplomas or troll dolls.
I shook them loose; I spurred them with the burr of success
to bless my coffee hour with brags of lust for power
and wondrous deeds "out there."

I am not ready to accept the notion
that I am, after all, a receptacle for half-used jogging shoes
and frayed turtlenecks while they, in bumptious nonchalance,
rattle off to battles of their own devising—until spring break.

Passages

The winds blow down from the glaciers.
Grasses and meadow rue push up
through the straw leavings and dung
of another season to find chill sunlight
for the ninety-day wonder of life.
Small birds stop off to fight each other
over a pinpoint gnat caught in a pine-needle net.
The siskins caw and feint at each other
with the swagger of small boys.

It is the switching time.
We are at the crossroads, the switchyard of the year.
The old are older. The young are older, too.
You and I are a bridge the young and old
cross over on their opposite ways.
They stop to wave, to pay the toll,
to blow a kiss, and away they go.

Because we are the ones standing still,
we see that the roads
will not cross again.

Montana Aurora

Wrapped in the comfortable fat of the Cadillac,
the old lady adventures 4 a.m.
toward rendezvous far away.
Here, towns are always far away.

Orion, so easily forgotten, scion of an unkempt sky,
is familiar in his orderly geometry,
reliable at such an hour.

Now, ten miles out, the sky explodes.
North toward heaven, it shudders
the orgasmic glee of space.
Ripples and currents undulate
in silent thunder and fluorescent waterfalls.
It must be the end of the world!

She is pinned to her seat.
The curtain is ripped away.
Half a sky flings serpentine rays,
a kaleidoscopic expansion.
There is no one to tell,
no one to beg for attention
to this blinkless extravagance,
no companion but the gasping wish for God.

She sees, in this moment, beyond the possible,
shot past all limits by her glimpse of eternity,
alone in the fear and rapture of meeting herself at last,
an unwilling witness to glory.

The Old Lady and the Ravens

for Norski

She'd lost her dog years ago,
giving him Viking rites on a snow mound
far away in the trees.
Once he had brought her a gift,
a dead raven's stinking wing,
and soon the ravens showed up.

They were there in the way of myth,
a network of black figures, smug
as if they'd seen woolly mammoths
on a regular basis.

She knew about ravens: They eat cardboard,
plastic straws, and dead hounds.
Like "Ilkley Moor," she thought, humming.
And the link was wrought.

They knocked their wooden noise out there,
xylophones of one tone, subtle,
as if she should knock two-by-fours in answer.

Coming home from work, she would see them
dip and soar over the old car,
then perch like sentinels,
mannerly and formal old monks,
their altar boys announcing her arrival.

They'd wait for hours, nights, frigid dawns,
draped at angles in stiffened trees.

"We have him, you know—
brain, heart, and those Viking eyes."
She began collecting garbage, school lunch leavings,
produce-bin discards in green buckets, hauling them,
dank and fetid in the old car, not enough
and something less than soup-line fare,
but a token, a gift, an offering.

She didn't dare a new hound, and knew they resented it,
but they made feast of these hors d'oeuvres,
for, after all, it takes thirteen years to stew an elkhound,
and ravens take their own time.

Bay by Bird Island

The old green boat had a flat bottom.
This new one, Viking-ribbed,
splits the wake neatly with its spine.
Riffles and bubbles, freak waves,
stir the lake in the wake
made by the insult of the motor.
We are used to it.
With medieval trumpets in fanfare
we arrive in the bay. Subtle is a word
this newcomer never knew.

We burned the old green boat.
Who would have thought the old man
had so much blood in him?
Sulphurous flames seared the rotting boards,
the pitch drizzled, making torches.
The guts smoldered for two days,
refusing to die discreetly.
The black patch on the beach
required burial itself.

Mercifully now the efficient motor stops.
We glide, bumping occasional archaeological stumps.
It will be an hour before the lake relaxes,
an hour of patience we cannot guarantee as we sit,
embarrassed by our silence.
Bubbles come up in carbonated surprise through the sand.
Seaweed, brocading the water, settles gently.
Minnows, the last to know,
dart in pattern under our shadow.

The big brown is onto us.
It will take half a day and twenty yards of line
to tempt him. In this game he holds all the aces.
Too bad we burned the old green boat
which knew that still waters run deepest,
that motors are meant for fools,
and that the seaweed owns the bay,
the hot sands belching anthems under the lake.

The Walk

Four lodgepoles, dead dinosaurs, lie as they fell.
Once they made a room.
We played there, dolls and blankets,
trudging up the hillside laden down like pioneers.

Up the hill the old path is gone.
Now a power line marches its sky-snake way
from pole to pole where siskins teeter,
a circus act.
I came here last along the edge of aspen
with her, the old lady, before her knees said no,
to smell the smoky crunch of leaves,
not so much to see the gold as just to prove we could.

Alone now, I hear green leaves quake their water tune.
A flicker warns the hillside.
Finches cluck to their young
to freeze until the danger's passed
as if I eat babies. At the outcrop
marmot sits, furry statue on the lichen,
his pig-eyes watching me as if I come,
as others have, to heave a rock
midway into his ghetto.
He waits. We stare each other down.
He gives way first, moves like a bag lady
into his hole to the middle of the earth.
Downhill, as I go, I feel his eyes,
his and dozens more, on my back.

The old path is a road now, tracks
where the utilitarian cherry picker

has masticated its way under the power line.
I leave the hill to the eyes,
knowing it belongs to the power rig
which does eat babies after all.

A New Old Sky

It seemed an intelligent thing in the afternoon,
the bumpy puddles tapped by unobtrusive rain,
an adventure to stay all night out there below the mountain.
The firelight would be the only light,
the last glow seen across the water.
"Look there," they'd say, amazed. "Someone
 is still at the lake so late in the season."

It seemed brave, but at five a.m.,
still dark, still wet, deserted,
it's become a foolish thing,
a lumpy thing below the ears
which listen for the silence, feeling the thousand eyes
of those who roam and nibble
in the dark.

One could use a great full moon just now
instead of that sharp slit
that pokes a half-hole in an unfamiliar sky,
a foolish thing beneath Orion and the Pleiades,
so close to one another as if harboring a secret
with the rustle of an unfamiliar wind
across the damp, dead leaves.

People belong in their starless beds
where five o'clock is something odd and useless.

Yet all the long drab day just south of consciousness
perches the knowing:
those stars hang there behind the blue all day
and wait for some wise fool at five a.m.
to find them out.

Closing the Cabin

It takes doing, like a plot, to be here alone.
The lake, glass smooth, tinkers with silence
but out there a fish flips. The shuttered cabins
are sleeping humped against the hill
in a stance of emptiness. I shudder at how natural it is
for them to wait, empty, mute, half the year.
Their vacant porches are mouths hanging open,
an embarrassment like gaping garage doors
on Sunday morning.

Wood is stacked about, and porch furniture,
stashed awry like cripples, looks haywire.
Clay pots are leaning under things, upside down.

Not quite alone, not yet.
From a Chevy 4x4, someone shoots a .22,
while out in the middle, a convoy of wise ducks
cruises in the wisdom of innocence like an oil slick
upon the water. Discouraged, the hunter rumbles off,
echoing rattles through the woods. Silence again.

Why is there so great a need to be here
in the ache of a lost summer, to walk
as if naked among the echoed mores of Julys,
to want some counterfeit joy in the absence of others?
Why do we seek this immaculate distance from intrusion
by those most like ourselves?

Alone, the memories are enough.

The Woodrat

The woodrat comes in with the wood, of course,
knowing we will be warm and full of nooks,
things to lug about, like cheap candies
and old bread left for the birds to haggle over.

We in our beds hear scufflings and a knock or two,
as with small quakes, sly rumblings and minor jolts,
beams creaking in bad humor, settling for a rotation.
Here we are in the bottom of a caldera.
We must be mad to be here at all,
and now the woodrat's with us.

It is fall, and a rat must make plans.
He takes a chance
leaving his mate out there to fend for herself.
She must wonder why she teamed up with an explorer,
but he seemed so stable and adoring
there in the kindling crate behind the logs,
frisking, preening his whiskers.

Now he is in the house,
scampering as best he can
with his summer belly hampering his jog
along the edges of the kitchen.
He is inconvenienced like a pedestrian
crossing against the light.
I am a Mack truck, so he avoids me under the sink.

They'll murder you, I think.
They always do. It's a duty of some kind.
We cannot keep a woodrat in the house, even here.

A trap,
a big thing with doors at each end,
a handle,
a marvel if one can make a rat go in.

He goes, to our relief,
his brief encounter over.
He leaves chips and dip, nuts and noodles.
He eyes us through the mesh
like Danton bound for the guillotine,
a captive swashbuckler with marvelous mustaches,
the round eyes of his kind, keen, wise, stoic.
He is shunted off to exile at the campground.

His mate, estranged, deserted,
with no pension, pregnant to boot,
leaves on Saturday for a better neighborhood.

Dragonfly

Against the screen a translucent fly,
he with exotic silken wings, retractable,
the shape of feathers,
patterned Japanese in light and silver,
circles round in dance, a Vivaldi allegretto,
a maypole pirouette
'round his own caught leg,
twirling on the twisted thing,
straining in the silence of entrapment,
braided to the screen by his own leg.

The Raven

Here the dead remain in position
like broken glass after a picnic:
the bat between the shutters,
the squirrel in the woodpile,
the shrew midway across the dock,
the robin drowned in the watering can.

The raven's position defies gravity—
splay-winged at the top of the fir,
audacious and expectant,
about to swoop, then soar as yesterday,
annoyed by swallows and stung by the bills
of siskins in rage.

But he is dead.
The wings are spread,
the head looks open-eyed at lake and sky
as he perches, a figure on the prow
of a Viking ship.

The wind does not dislodge him.
Needles have sewn him to the branch;
spiders stitch him in gossamer to the conifer,
like lace.

This grace he never displayed before.
He is captured mid-flight, a muted kite.
How was it he managed ascension?
What boost made this last sortie, airborne to the top,
a will of extremes?

Next summer will his white bones
and winter-whipped feathers remain there,
a Jolly Roger waiting to fall like jackstraws,
as impermanent as the others who lie gently
until the earth heaves
and even itself forgets?

Below the Wasatch Front

TV dawn across the Intermountain West is color-adjustable.
Reds chase orange. More purple for the Voice.
Here it comes, modulated and seductive,
indecent for God. It is a hired voice,
a gospel according to Heston,
dubbed like poster paint on the black and white screen.

The History of the Saints
making the desert bloom like a rose
in Imax proportions.
Much black on white for the Wasatch;
much white on black for the Temple construction, 1853.
Color returns as the sweet matron
with her brood of five is interviewed among late marigolds.
Too small a house for too many children,
though she didn't mean it to come out that way.

Maps now. The Wasatch Front is a war zone,
pins angling toward the South, Cedar City to Vegas.
Laughs all around; who would believe
the Saints settled Las Vegas?
Mammon, maybe, or Baal.
Great names for a dance team.

Ignored St. George, suitable now for golf and trailers.
After God and before air conditioning,
a summer hell where the Giant Joshua
plucked off the children,
crying for forbidden water,
dying with swollen tongues
and questions where the eyes should be.
Tactless of me to remember.

The Lion of the Lord sent my great ones there,
reprieved from the smoky Midlands,
off the boat like cattle,
only to be given the dubious choice:
          St. George or hell.

They made the wrong choice,
and now, forgotten, they lie forever
under the white on white of old tombstones
in an alien desert of red hills and heat waves
where now I imagine the Grandmother
brooding in everlasting sorrow
while the whites of golf balls
hum through the Imax desert.

Itinerant Photographer at the Ranch, 1883

The girl sits with folded hands
as ladies should. Her eyes, leaking stories,
plead toward the hidden camera
where two splayed legs, suggesting rapture,
arch behind a tripod, the black tent undulating
as if holding doomed kittens,
hiding all but the cyclops of the lens.
Her black gown, resurrected for the occasion,
poses its wrinkles for the indifferent eyes
of a century hence.

The ample lady, sitting now, defies the camera to tell
how many mistakes she baffles in this moment.
She will not let her look betray
the error of this place.
This is her public look, ready on demand.
Her gambled choices must not now show forth
when all there is lies mirrored in this image.

The other, an aunt perhaps,
the chaff of the drought,
always an extra, the throwaway,
for once part of the family,
for they cannot name her burden,
wishes for fire or quake to let her run.
She looks beyond the lens for some escape
or better yet, the sudden levitation
of a virgin ascending.
Her corner of the photo droops,
defying balance and symmetry.
She does not fit, never did, never will.
Oh-God-why-am-I-here?

Of the four, the rotund man hides best
for he has whiskers.
He stands behind as if to prevent escape.

These, his women, are all he shows
of the hollow wind, the withered grass,
the stillborn calf, the endless snow,
flash powder sealing all there is of him.

Old Wife's Tale

Before she became a statistic
she was the second wife of a polygamist,
and nine babies later,
she sickened. She pulled up the comforter
and wouldn't get out of her bed.

The bearded one was an adventurer,
seeing the desert lands
with the blindness of the bluegrass exiles.
He walked over the Comstock Lode
knowing it was holy ground
no good for corn.

This unexpected night was frantic
with lights in every window.
He carried his burdensome conscience
into the parlor, pontificating
on the expense of coal oil.
She died anyway, to his surprise.
It was not expedient.

It is doubtful she welcomed him
out of the dark.

After the Auction

As if the wind had changed and now the air were clearer,
after dust and lace and plush had settled into hiding,
all that was left were the gold-edged mirror
and the photo albums full of cross-eyed babies
no one could remember,
babies glorious in christening gowns,
the mothers tightly laced, uncles gazing sermons
from above long, well-coiffed beards,
pious Mormons, having crossed the plains and mountains,
to find, alas, no precious fountain of youth,
but all the same, a life at last of porches, hedges,
and leatherbound volumes of home remedies.

No one really wanted the embarrassing photos.
Something sad settled in as we, amused,
pictured the fat and pompous uncle, the one
with the watch chain strung tight across his middle,
gracing a bar, perhaps, in vulgar anonymity
or staring across the sanitary tiles
of McDonald's Downtown.

Indian Summer

Logan, Utah, 1935

The Bannock women came once a year,
a cyclical phenomenon like batches of blackbirds
or boxelder bugs, suddenly everywhere, endured
by the mothers.

    The fathers were never home
    when they came.

They came in pairs or threes
with paper sacks held under their blanket flaps
like handbags to be thrust forward by brown hands
toward the mothers who wore flowered housedresses.

    The fathers would have said belittling things
    or pretended not to be at home.

The women were mute except to say "sugar"
in listless voices, eyes to the sand.

    The mothers, knowing well the ritual,
    would eye us to take care and watch,
    for Indians were habitual thieves, like gypsies.

      The fathers were changing tires
      or delivering cleaning as if the Depression
      had never happened.

The women retrieved the sacks in silence,
turning like hippos in water,
clutching the booty under the blankets,
and moving on heavy legs down the street.

The mothers looked relieved and went
back to ironing percale sheets with G.E. irons.

    "The squaws came today," the fathers would hear,
    and they offered up silent thanks that they
    were fathers and did not have to deal with such.

The next day we put on car robes and feathers,
and went from house to house
with empty paper sacks like Hallowe'en.
It was an old game.

Ritual

After tea she would leave to dress.
It was the powdering time of the afternoon,
and she would let me watch.

She was flat as a board,
her breasts like empty marble bags,
linen-like under the false pink of the powder.
She bound her wrinkled softness into a corset
reminiscent of a tennis shoe's midsection,
canvas with ribs askew,
the dangling garters rattling like wind chimes.
She hunched her narrowed shoulders
to let shallow bits of herself settle into empty spaces,
pushing her gentlenesses into its rigid shape
the way I'd seen her tamp dough
into the corners of bread pans.

She pulled on cotton stockings and a dress
whose lines were bent and tugged
by the ribbed forms of stress beneath it.

I waited for the last, the best,
when she poked around a tiny box
and found the earrings,
diamonds in gold Tiffany settings.
They stood out from her narrow earlobes
like twin headlights.
She could push them through the puckered tunnels
without looking.
I'd catch my breath, waiting for blood to spurt.

She told me again how the first needle went through,
pulling a blue silken ribbon,
how each day they'd jerk the silk
until at last the tiny holes healed.
"I fainted once," she said
as the diamonds glittered their magic bond between us
in the dusty afternoon.

Tea with Grandmother Horlick

She wore her apron and a hat
as side by side we sat in rockers
on the porch behind ivy and wandering jew
to drink our tea.
Hers was thick with sugar,
mine a sea of blue milk.

"It was a wonderful house, new," she said,
and the glow that came from ancient pride
intensified as if the scorekeeper there inside
were listening once again for her approval.
She would not slide past the buffets of the sixty years
that house had stood.

"Brick," she'd say again.
They all were brick, I knew, for I'd been
victim to this tale a thousand times.
"Yes, brick," I'd help. "Not adobe."

"Adobe was good, but, well, more crude.
Now the old house, there on the corner,
that's adobe with walls twelve inches thick."
She could not hide a speck of pride
which that house, too, the old one there,
had earned from her as if to share the stage
in this ceremonial recital.

"But the brick one, this one, you see," and
her voice trailed off to let the rocker hum,
    creak here, ease there,
"You see," she said to someone out there who

more often joined us those days, the someone whom
she listened to, a small smile across her shiny dentures,
"You see," and this made all the difference,
"this house was for me."

CCC, 1933

I

The camp was in a field of wild high grass.
The barracks topped the hill.
A road passed here, a pair of ill-matched ruts
too narrow and too wide for wheels to fit.

Old boys and old men came from cities—
Chicago, New York—
to this unlikely hummock, thin-skinned over rock
amid wild wheat, pocked with gopher holes.
Not a dime in their pockets, we heard,
but then, who needed dimes in this forgotten boondock
where nothing served to fill a Saturday night
before a dreary Sunday?

A dollar a day and enough to eat,
sweet enough promise to bring them to this hill,
strangers to sagebrush and
the shrill cry of Cooper's hawk.

Between the rains of June,
the dust blew like the Kansas
they had never seen.
Strange to them the rumble
as tractors bludgeoned roads through the pines,
the crash of trees, mud-splat, a stuck truck,
boom of dynamite,
the rush and muck of making more mud roads
across the meadows thick with wild geraniums.

"Hey, what would you give for a beer back home
in some old alley between two brick walls?"

II

One young boy from Jersey, with an axe,
hacked, missed, and placed the steel
deep into his shin. No real doctor about,
my father asked to look into that hole of blood
and pulsing muscle, rent and slashed.
He, with aplomb, when no one else was willing,
pulled and taped, then wrapped the ragged gash.

"You are a doctor, we have heard,"
the white-faced street boy prayed aloud.
And though he said, "Oh, no," my father,
before that panicked glaze-eyed crowd,
somehow put that bandage so,
and gave that alien boy
some hope to lean upon.

By fall they'd gone,
as if by edict. Gone the fence,
the barracks, planks, the water tanks.
Only the roads remained. We never knew
which man it was who came back through
with wife and child and jagged scar
to tell of grim days when hard luck
carried him here for a dollar a day.

The Biggest Man in the World

Way back before the Guinness books,
when the finest thing at the fair
was the freak show, and
    Slitzy-the-Pinhead
 came back the next year as
    The Last of the Aztecs,
Robert Wadlow came to our town,
advertised by Mr. Rechow's shoe store,
a cheap alternative to Tom Thumb,
Elephant Man, or ShirleyTemple.

Sprawled as if dropped there from Dorothy's house,
he iced the top of Mr. Rechow's Ford,
one leg foundered like a log on the right fender,
the other on the left, his heft
draping itself in folds of casual abandon.
Atop his Gulliver's head,
squashed rakishly to one side over an ear
as big as a bagel was a fedora,
specially made by a tent company.
A white lobster of a hand rested on his knee.
He had five fingers.
    I counted them.

The crowd milled. Traffic detoured.
Some people laughed,
self-conscious as peeping toms.
Men spat and women giggled.
    "Will you look at that! He's a freak!"
someone announced loudly,
apparently assuming a man that big
must also be stone deaf.

We walked around the parked Ford, ogling our fill.
On his back was a stitched label,
    KENNER'S SOLES MAKE YOU STAND TALL
That close, we could see his eyes,
patient, like those of the farmers who sat on benches
while their wives were busy coveting in Penney's.

Somebody said,
    "Bet there's a flood when he pees."
Wadlow pretended not to hear.
Maybe he *was* deaf, after all.
    "How do you suppose he . . . "
and that became everything: cars, beds,
chairs, urinals, ceilings, elevators, girls.
Suddenly I was embarrassed.
I wished he hadn't come
and told my mother so.

    "At least he's not in the fair," she said.
    "Besides, he'll die young.
    Something always goes wrong.
    You know," she added,
    "we really should get your oxfords resoled."

The Bull

Father,
one day when I really didn't know about bulls,
we saw one, a Hereford, a huge bulbous bell-ringer hulk
alone in the feedlot by the highway,
posed in a classic billboard stance on the raked manure,
waiting for love or execution, whichever came first,
though I didn't know that then;
honestly, Father, I didn't know.
So I said, as the car whizzed past the white fences,
making checkerboards of the afternoon sunlight,
I said, carefully because I was alone with you,
a happening strange and rare,
making both of us self-conscious, I said,
"What do they use bulls for,
because they don't give milk,
and we don't eat them, do we?"
The child I was asked.

You looked confused and troubled,
as if we were having a flat tire
or should have picked up that fellow on the overpass
who was picking his teeth with a piece of straw.

You waited and I waited.
I remember it so well because
I knew I had said something wrong,
and I wondered what it was I must do.
I did, we both did, the only thing we could do
when we were alone, which was almost never:
we did nothing.

But all these years later,
whenever I see the barns and the fields
of Angus and Santa Gertrudis,
I think how sad it is that we cannot talk together now
when I don't care about bulls but wish instead for you,
wish I could breathe life into our billboard rapport
which never moved into reality,
wish I could say something marvelous,
whatever that might be.

Impromptu Dump

Among the Engelmann spruces,
inside their roots, cans rot.
Tennis shoes and a Pennzoil plastic bottle
make a collage of junk. Skunks
and chipmunks do-si-do amid the rubbish
which deer by miracle avoid with dainty steps.
Pack rats ransacked this melange
long ago.

Ashamed, the grasses kink toward each other,
having cannibalized the cardboard box years ago.
It is like finding the skeleton
of an old pet, collar, chain,
nail clippers, the clippings,
and the brush. Dried bones.
It is who we were.

I remember your stopping the car,
idling the engine,
lifting out the cardboard box,
walking resolutely into the trees,
and throwing a winged clatter of cans,
a spray of catsup bottles,
a cacophony of trash.

Remember the useless old stove
which sits out eternity
on the bottom of the lake,
leaching itself into anonymity?

All that you left me to remember
has been spent, used up,

stashed, forgotten.
The photographs of the races,
the old boots, a medal or two,
your memoirs (10¢ at the thrift store),
the wheelbarrow rusting under the porch.
This is your Tutankhamen disarray:
refuse refusing to sink back into the earth,
as enduring as the deserted oil refinery at Kevin
where oil-slick puddles ripple in the wind.

The Widow

I

They try. They are dears,
but it is over.

They say it is better this way,
buttering over the open wound
as best they can.

They say I wouldn't want you now,
maimed, crippled, chaired, unfocused,
bedded, blubbering, stuttering, grunting.

They cannot know, nor should they,
that I would take you back
any way at all.

II

They say time heals.
Well, it doesn't.
Who are these sages
who go by "they"?
Where do they come from, anyway,
to be our sacrosanct judges?

You left without a backward look.
There in our bed, you were dead,
and not a word of why.
In those last few moments,

did you not dare wake me?
What would you have said
in that last minute of our life together?
How could you leave,
knowing I would lie forever and forever
wondering?

Can time heal that?

The Mallard

She never cried but once after the child.
Perhaps something dried up.
We wondered about it.

Only once, that day when the tractor came,
the summer of the trench through the snowberries,
the summer the mallard nested close, the fool.

She knew the mallard was there,
silly and brave on her nest.
We had orders to detour.
The path was blocked by stones.

Over her dishpan she saw the tractor
churning up the hill,
chewing a path through the bushes.

Running as her hands dripped suds for tears,
she screamed against the noise.
The duck flew up, beating for space with its wings.

The eggs were gone in the shambles of mud and twigs.
She folded to the ground and wept aloud
while all of us watched in astonishment.

Full Circle

We spent so much time missing him,
our weekdays were diversions,
dances around empty Sundays,
only the funny stories fair game.
"Dad always" or "Dad never,"
but mostly Dad didn't
die. Not really. We wouldn't let him.
We didn't know how.

She told me I looked like him.
I wondered about it.
He had muscles that rippled like an oryx,
a nose that followed the contours of old wrecks,
teeth that turned brown like his skin.
The skin, yes. We were both mistaken for Navajos.
The sun made us the color of chestnuts.

She wouldn't know me now—
the chestnuts having faded,
the counterfeit muscles tipsy on the ice,
the face around the mouth unsure—
for at long last
I am beginning to look like her.
They all say it as if it were a surprise.

Somewhere, quietly, the two of them
are turning into twins.

The Harvest

Sideways she eyes me as I open the can,
surprising her with grape juice.
Inside are purple bubbles, rich and runny.
The spill is a subtle stain cleaving to the sink
with permeating royal-cloth ink and smear.

"Canned juice always stains," she announces
as if "rain rains," and "pain pains."
"I like my own better," she adds, postscript,
the needed quip of judgment.
Warily I pour the chemical marvel,
purple and identical to her own
but that these grapes have not sat,
dripping to her vat from the flour bag
sagging from the open window all the night,
drip, drip, dripping to purple light,
dawn's ooze of color, spattering spill
on screen and glass and sill,
a nectar catalyst between us.

But she will not drink this, taking tea instead,
for, tender as these grapes have been,
they have not gone through ritual
of wash and pick and skin.
Other hands, somehow unclean,
have picked and packed and marred
the beauty of the vineyard,
shutting the sweetness in tin,
not boiled as bottles are,
nor lined up, row on row,
abundance in the afternoon sunshine.

The Bivalves: Widow's Bric-a-Brac

I

Single bivalve oxymoron,
the blue vase (fluted edge) sits singly,
in a dignity of solitude.

> Like Sotheby's, you cataloged:
> it was a wedding gift,
> circa 1884, one of a pair. The
> sister took hers to California
> where she broke it.

II

Wanton in opulence,
cherubs perch in perpetual flutter,
coy in redolence of Dresden violets,
chubbed in folds of flesh
like new-made sausages,
their gaze through the candles
on squatted legs of china
resting on the nothing nearby.

> You said the maid dropped one;
> the rich aunt fired her. Both
> maids and candelabra went out of style,
> just as did rich aunts.

III

Red Ridinghood, frozen in medieval bisque,
her dolorous face benign,
an unglazed arm guarding the basket,

as if that, silly girl, were what he coveted,
gazes with frozen courage
into his canine adoration,
the virgin and the carnivore,
duo eternal in porcelain–almost.
Alas. His ear is gone,
relegating them forever to
the status of semi-trash.

Like taking in orphans, you wrapped her up,
leaving the other, Bo-Peep in her bisque paddock
with a perfect sheep, to the rightful heirs.

> You said every time as you dried it,
> "One of a pair,"
> the bivalve part of you
> begrudging the absence of heat
> in the universe.

Autumn Day

In the pinkness of the autumn morning
the man shaving paused to look at his face
in the square of the mirror,
knew that he was not going to live forever,
and decided he would plant trees.
He must plant trees.

In the silver of the autumn noon,
sweating,
he dug and buried the stubbornesses of lodgepole roots,
hearing his heart pump over the sound of the soft wind.
Then he went back to securities of one kind or another.

In the brass of two o'clock
the old lady, following his muddy tracks,
took her trowel and dug up the baby trees,
casting them into the lake,
knowing that she would live forever
and that they would grow to hide her view of the world.

In the gold of the afternoon
the telephone company,
which had already proved that it would live forever,
came to bury the line, churning up the yard,
bringing the good news that both of them were wrong,
but they would be able to phone in the verdict,
should there be a change of plans.

Robin Hood

With autumn, something primordial,
subancestral, genetic,
rose to the surface.
She, protected, pampered, Edwardian
by rearing and admonishment,
became to our astonishment of late,
a thief.

And bold.

Leaves blowing, to her, were the symbol of knowing
that gathering and stowing against winter must cuckold
the cold.

It was a game of wits.
One at a time she rolled logs in random sizes,
too large for her strength,
then covering her tracks, put them in stacks
where through winter they'd wait, mute,
comforting, potential, essential, ready.
She held within her the mindless hoarding of the squirrel.

Daily the woodpile grew, and
we knew.
To confront her was too blunt, too direct, destructive
to that fragile grasp with which she clung to warmth,
that hold.

She spirited small ends of pine and spruce
to the pile near the porch by little red wagonfuls.
By leaps and heaps the pile grew.

They knew now, those neighbors.
Their smiles gave in to condescension,
to lifted eyebrows and chuckles.
The secret was out. Poor dear.
Aunt Beth steals wood.

Was there more warmth in stolen wood,
some good in cheating one more time against the frost,
against the beating of wings against the window
in winter twilight?

Divestiture

The car went first.
She gave the violets to the minister's wife,
the geraniums to the priest,
her cat to the garbage man.

She thought long of the rocks,
the obsidian, quartz, the fool's gold.
In this Indian country, the things of this world
were shared, not owned,
but these rocks were hers.

It was like packing to go to heaven.
She could no longer gather, only divest.
She found a rock-garden person
from the other end of town.
When he came to haul the rocks
into a new career of obscurity,
to sink abysmally into the sod beneath his junipers,
she, the acolyte, cradled each to his truck
as a sacrifice.
"This one," she whispered, "came from Silver Gate,
and this one came from Yellowstone!"
She stood straight for this last slap at the law.

Her other rocks, less contraband, were left behind,
hunched into an eternity of their own,
gravestones for the pansies
which would die of thirst now anyway.

Slipping at the Opera

Our common grounds were the moments
which none of the others understood.
I was always breathless with you because
our four feet made the same track
at the same cadence.
Mother and daughter, we were together
because we were one.
Hardly ever does that happen.

Now it doesn't happen at all.

We are on either-other sides of the river,
you and I, once of the water together,
separate currents now on diverse sides of the island.

Wagner, all the schmaltz, the pizazz,
the hums, the yes-yes-yes-there-it-is,
now as I watch and listen, I have alone,
as if deaf, only closed captions for song.

You doze.
You snort awake to the bobbings and squabblings
of birds at the free lunch.
You blink at the surprise of sunlight and the wind
and whatever caprice you see
in the cloud's pas de deux,
but you miss the crescendos and the grand finales.
You tired of the common ground.

Instead, you are outside on the roof,
looking in at a dusty window upside down,

clinging to the sill by your bent fingernails,
the curtain switching its gossamer hypnosis
before your eyes.
The tunes, the harmonies, have lost the track.
The groove dissolves.
You cannot jump the ice cakes anymore.

Your tickets are for bad seats in the back row,
the *Liebestod* lost, Isolde resurrected to cheering
while you hunt for your cane under the seat.

Long Distance

The telephone man goes everywhere,
including the sanitary old folks home
where tawdry old ladies are tied to their chairs,
upright like rag dolls, all eyes and slumps.
Bobby socks and slippers sporting roses and gum soles
are tacked to purple legs, tent poles holding up
the blue transparencies of their bag selves.
Housecoats flap about, picked by their picking fingers.
But it is the eyes that get him.

He fiddles and fumbles with the cords
of the useless phones,
plugging them into the real places
where no one answers,
fixing them to ring frenetically
from someone out there.

The ladies cannot reach the phones.

The telephone man, a savior wearing AT&T on his back
with his sack of efficiency and splices,
looks down at the gum soles,
for he cannot meet the eyes.

"Let me go," she pleads from the Dachau of her chair.
"Let me loose." And she plucks his sleeve.
He puts the phone next to her.
"See there. You can call out now,"
and the triumph of science makes him smile.
She plucks at the restrainer,
the new word for hell,
then says through her rattling teeth,
"I am going home soon.
Call and tell them that."

Subterfuges

In this business of waiting for her to die
we have perfected strategies,
notably the sidelong glance.
We have learned to listen to wheezing,
the rattle under the coffee cup,
though she pretends it doesn't happen,
hiding the hiss.

The glance, our watching,
is like the walk-about which ravens do
while the coyote takes his first pick
at the corpse,
the patience in case he drops a rib
or turns to sniff the air.

Our blinkless glance sees through this act
like solving sleight-of-hand tricks.
It is a kind of waiting. It is a kind of dread.

If she should look up to catch us
at our penetrating search,
we would be found wanting,
as if spying at a thief's first pocket-picking
when we wondered if what we saw was real.
We would glow red with shame for having noticed.

At St. Joseph's

Nuns cry simply. No mascara runs.
Tears leave no river marks in powder.
It is a cleansing thing.
They weep for the dead and for the living
and those between, for all are one.

Sister Mary of the Sorrows weeps,
letting her tears splotch her charts.
Her round Celtic eyes swim in blue saucers,
her woe surprising in this place
where no one breathes out of tune,
for fear of drawing attention,
and death nods with the tick of every clock.

The grieving man stands silent,
a funeral spray in his arms,
a gaucherie of gladiolas for the survivors.
Even the ribbons don't ruffle an inch of Sister's habit.
"Thank you," she says.
He is relieved to be rid of it
and melts into the maw of the elevator.

Later she pulls the spray apart,
nosegays for the breakfast trays.

Geraniums

The geraniums grew old in mismatched terra-cotta,
rangy, tough, gnarled.
Incongruous blooms made surprises,
no purples or blues,
but might as well have been.

Every day the old lady picked off yellow leaves.
Her fingers, moving like spiders
among the stinking stalks,
fused into a fasces the knots, knobs, and veins.
She counted the blooms every day.
Nobody checked up.

When she left everything—
her bed, her joy, her mind—
she would not leave the clay pots of wrinkled color.
They went along with the pills and the cane
to clutter, drip, impose,
clutching with her an illusive patience
in the confines of one room,
perching like chickens near the window,
waiting for the sun to warm them.

After her, they are the first to go.
They sit in the garage, freezing in the dark,
shrinking, dying of thirst and gloom,
dangling their peppery leaves in brittle dejection,
stiffening comments on the vicissitudes of age,
wondering why nobody comes to give them decent burial
under the snow.

In the Absence of a Will

She went without baggage,
no toothbrush, no comb and curlers,
left her rings behind.

She left in no ethereal ascension
but left part of herself with her curlers,
scorning the utterly spiritual
by leaving the rings where she hid them.

Her leavings
made us look into each other's eyes with guilt,
for who was I to take her rings from under the highboy
and who was he to toss her toothbrush,
comb, and curlers into the trash
as if they burned at the touch?

The dump is, at the last, where one's fortification
against a rainy day goes,
where curlers collapse in the mighty compactor
and finally lose their ability to haunt.

The Letters

After her death, we put the letters in a bag.
It took up the floor of a closet
and was difficult to ignore.

Later,
I took the bag to the bed and dumped them out.
Many were from me to her, sophomoric things:
gee-whiz, sometimes in purple ink.
I remembered them vaguely;
they seemed written by someone else in my handwriting.
She had kept them all in their dated envelopes
as if they might be important someday.

One small one was from my father
when she was an army bride
living off the base in Tacoma,
a note saying he would see her Saturday
and to be ready.
It was full of urgency,
not at all like the other letters she had kept.

I was embarrassed.
They had been lovers, and I had not noticed.

I burned it with the rest in the stove that very day,
bag and all.

The Other Side

At times she gave an Indian's gaze
to the mountains.
I wondered what it was she saw.
Her small smile seemed focused,
but often as not, she linked with the top,
ten thousand feet up, buzzing a kinship,
vague, myopic, through a haze of woodsmoke,
or,
inward as if seeing love, over the edge of horizon,
the other side.

Now I find myself gazing at dusk,
pushing my attention to the other side,
beyond the sound of birds, trucks, voices,
waiting to hear the news, lakes
where thaw means only August,
and dust may sit forever undisturbed
as it did before the Moonwalk.

There is news,
but I cannot hear it.

The Antisocial Norm

This is what I wanted.
This is where I want to be.
Alone.

Not really alone, not for a long time,
not all night, not deserted, maimed, cast off,
not betrayed or sold out,
not widowed, not destitute
to sleep, shivering in a doorway
or over an iron grate,
not hiding out in the restroom
of some obscure dive. No.
None of these.

But this: alone in the house,
on the rooftop,
behind a tree in the yard,
under the stereo,
inside the refrigerator,
twirling with the fan,
here.

I have waited for the last to leave.
Now I lock the door. No music,
lest someone guess—
a Fuller Brush man, a *Watchtower* zealot,
a lost tourist who thinks I'm a condominium.
The phone is off the hook.

It is a fanatical thing—like needing a drink.
I must have it.

I don't want to listen, to nod, to plan,
to clean the hydrator, not now.
I want to be the town at four a.m.,
just here, intact, same size, same shape,
but for now, responsible to nobody's stomach,
to be theme with no variations, just this . . .
        until noon.

Art Show

I look at the paintings
and do as I should.
I back away; I tilt the head;
I put my glasses against the chin,
considering carefully by a criterion
which isn't there. Free coffee doesn't help.

I move back to the watercolor of the wet sheep
because I understand it.
It is a wet sheep.

The sheep has had a bath he doesn't want.
He drips on the concrete floor,
ears low like French farmhouse roofs
sorry about the weather.

I move away to the Bay of Acrylics,
I try the exploding poppies
but they elude me.
I study a torn ceramic package
feeling the vandalism of my confusion.
I know that it will place. It does. Fourth.

The wet sheep wins.
I know it isn't the best painting.
The judge knows it too, but
perhaps he is intimidated.
He makes a nice speech to the forty-nine
who didn't win
a thousand dollars.

I am vindicated—yet
the only thing I really know is
that the sheep is sad.

Easter Snow

No sunset. Socked in. Wet.
Evening snow comes in day-glow,
up from under, sideways,
almost upside down, against everything;
sticky on the glass, sticky on the walls,
sticky on itself, an insult against the sill.

But out there I hear a bird's call,
strident, insistent, shrill, persistent.
A clarion woodpecker works his fretful way
up a wet trunk, moving out of sync.

He is like a man I knew.
His walk was a single lurch,
disjointed, his wishbone body saying,
"Cling to ourselves. All together now, move!"
Swaying, he often fell,
and when he fell, he'd laugh,
though in the end they found him in his closet,
his Tinkertoy body swinging gracefully
from an extension cord
wrapped neatly around his neck.

Now crazybird hunts and pecks
as if this were a July evening,
his bill a riveter, rat-a-tat-tat.
He seems not to know that it is snowing,
that it is too wet for bugs.

Anasazi Rain

When it rains like this,
kissing the windows like audible lovers,
reaching,
then rushing straight,
like a charwoman's haphazard swipes at shift's end;

when it rains this way,
scattering me to shelter
under the lip of the slab at Hovenweep,
gathering my Anasazi knees into myself,
hoarding the wet in my ears
as do the pocks in the stones,
saucering the drops for an hour,
making or breaking lizard-lives
between cloudbursts and coyotes;

it is then that my feet take root.
My body sways,
tries to turn the black of lodgepole trunks,
turns face to the wet, throat roaring the thunder,
at-one-ment.

When it rains, rains, rains like this,
oh, run, picnickers,
giggle your way into wet ruins,
cling in your dripping shelters,
leave me to imagine the suckling desert
while these rivulets smear my fake window,
and my real roots cling to the tiring earth,
tied tendrils to the immaculate random of this place
where it rains and rains and rains.

The Road under My House

No one remembers what road it was
from where to where my house sits on.
Snow melts freshets in its ruts
washing out the seeds of things,
sprucing up the careless obsidian sand,
polishing the quartz again,
so there it is, a stubborn trail.

Clover seeds, a tree or two,
reluctant where this road holds on,
move out after awhile to show
they find no comfort there.

Each year we scratch, we plant and urge.
Sparse grass and aspen bend,
turning their heads away.
A fence puts out that this is not a road.

But at night I think soft sounds
of moccasins pat down the sand
in Nez Perce patience
to move my house away.

Eight A.M.

What used to be the slapdash exit,
grabbing toast and coat at once,
now is a measured minuet
into the world whose grooves
are worn and polished by habit.

Thermos, handbag,
pocket flasks of courage,
all held tightly underarm,
at alarm, we sally forth
into that slot of hours.

I have been there before.

What do they see?
    The early evidence of emery board,
    the bow beneath the collar tied
    in brave bouffant designed to hide
    the double chin, but there,
    that softness slips to south,
    pulls down the pinnings of the mouth.

Carefully, brown spots are covered.
Curls and gray-tipped mat above the ears
are gently pushed and puffed and patted.

Dear God, no wind, please.

Upstairs

They wonder what I look at
when I stand so long at the window.
I must focus on something soon,
no moon, too obvious in the afternoon,
but some bogus wonder like a flamingo.
That would do it.

If they ask, I shall say
I see flamingos, not these poor cold-fluffed juncos.
They would not see why
I should look so long at slate-colored juncos.
Bunk, they would say, and why don't I sit down.

"How pretty," I will say to no one special.
How pretty could mean the snow which never melts,
the moon which has not risen for weeks and weeks,
or how pretty the flamingos
there among the snow-covered stones.

I cannot tell them about the ghost behind the tree.

Pending

It is healthy to have your life threatened.
Me, worried? Look at it this way:
I'm riding on this old spaceship
with the redwoods and the bristlecone pines,
and they don't look to be in such great shape either.

Or,
how many one-hundred-year-old women
have you seen lately?

Nevertheless,
how else would I have noticed
that paintbrush comes in lavender?
Why else would I have counted the stars in Orion
or listened all night for the coyote,
or known the smell of the elk wallow,
or watched the roll of the breathing, winded horse
at ten thousand feet?

When your life is threatened
you go to the top of the world to listen very carefully
to the love song of your own heart.

Real Estate at Portal Creek

A discovery demands some kind of commitment.
It will be an antidote for ache.

I will come back and say, "One day
I sat upon that rock, a boulder
big as the kitchen table.
I ran my fingers along its varicose veins
and picked at its liver-spot lichen."
I will think of it buried under snow and moonlight,
sheltering the thimbleberry,
waiting.

Where the road snakes across the clear-cut,
there I sink to ankle in water under ferns,
eat the stingy wild strawberry,
plan where to put my house.
Here is the Ansel Adams view.
I could lower the house by helicopter,
commute by snowmobile on sunny days.
All things are possible,
and it will be mine.

My other houses perch
on the edge of the Grand Canyon,
and on a knob near Carrot Basin,
and just below Going-to-the-Sun Highway,
and there, through the fence at Butchart Gardens.

From Portal Creek I take a small stone
with a red vein running through it
to place with my other real estate
under the stairs.

After the Walk

The words are catalog for loss
as if these roots, these freckled leaves
were those I saw in that old June
when everything was young,

as if, because they grasp the earth
their clutch has never yet been loosed
by doe, nor winter, nor fire, nor wheels,
nor these, my waffled feet.

Only the rocks and I are old,
and,
of all this matted hillside,
only I have changed.

Horse Butte

In a perpendicular neighborhood
a round mountain is good for grass.
Cows graze there occasionally
but "horse" sounds better.
No one remembers what the Bannock called it
when dogs pulled their travois
toward the giant spring.

Ten thousand years ago the butte
was the trash heap of a glacier,
rounded like the egg of the mind,
the dump of the ice-blender,
stirred by the random joke machine.
Time to redecorate, time to rearrange:
put the pink ones with the black ones,
polish them.
Five thousand years and the patina dazzles.

After the next ice overhaul,
someone might find one of my teaspoons
and gasp at the versatility of the aborigines.
The cemetery could be upended sacrilegiously.
My hip bone might have the power to age God
by a million years.
Horse Butte could move to St. Louis
to dam the Missouri.

Scheduling is sketchy at this point.

Fire Danger
Yellowstone, 1988

The harvest moon sets before dawn,
orange, grotesque in bulging nearness,
a message that it is the earth which moves
while the Great Pumpkin sulks behind foreign mountains
all my hidden day, fretting in somebody's night.

The neighbor's gray skulker cat sneaks in the half-light
toward the wayward night birds,
two ends of a day moving both ways.
Now at eve, the sun repeats the act,
gloomed by smoke to its moon-sister's size,
visible and naked through an editing of murk
to an equality,
an exposure in all its fury to a rationality of nearness
as if it too had been walked upon.

This is what fire does to me,
the gift of Prometheus whose despair
gave only one chance.
This pink and fetid film, housing retardants and fear,
paints the sky with the stink of smoke,
the message one of vulnerability and holocaust
where side by side glow conflagration
and the jar's only gift.

The Firehole

Once a great fire burned the lodgepoles,
swept the land and left it the firehole
out of which the new grew from ashes, a phoenix.

You in this place, this bowl of sand,
boiled and stewed by the rumbling furnace,
ground into diamonds of white and black
by the restless rivers of ice,
you who crisscross the age-old scars of the seas
and the lakes through which the dinosaurs slogged,
you, put your ear to the ground.

Do you feel it poised, pivotal, pulsating?
Do you wait for earth to shake and groan
with the pangs of birthing the peaks
to the skies above this basin of fragile crust?
Do you hear the hiss of the stewing steam
trapped in the rocks, seeking the daylight
like Merlin in his cave?

Do you feel the closeness of the center of the earth,
fire and ice, and the soft sound of moccasins?

Listen!

Meteor Shower

Under the shower of meteors in the August night,
the pit glows red, filled as it is with logs burning hot.
The people dug the pit and roasted a pig,
shredded and sauced it for their friends.
Now they are munching on it,
being careful not to spill sauce on the grass.
Somebody says it would be a real barbeque
if Herbie fell into the pit,
and they all laugh.

Under the shower of meteors
the man who reads the newspaper even on vacation
says that astronomers have discovered
another solar system.
The lady in green is vaguely vexed,
for she has not found it easy to remember
the names of the planets in this one.

Those who cannot eat all their portion of pig
put pieces in a plastic bag to take along.
One lady looks with awe
at the maroon sluggishness in the bag, saying,
"Whatever did we do
before Edison invented plastic bags?"
Everyone thinks of this carefully
for it seems a deep and truthful problem in the firelight.

Under the shower of meteors, the people drive home,
facing the comforting lights of the oncoming cars
until the neon of the town fills the sky.

Phaeton

Too fast he's past me like a bullet in his pickup.
Rain spatters my windshield while he,
in his role-play leather jacket, passes me with the racket
of tire, metal, and steel.

I hang on to my stalled steering wheel
as a splat of mud and wet drapes across the wiper pattern.
I am sitting still. I have run out of gas.

I see him reel, then brake,
a lurch across the highway, fluid and syrupy
through the rain, his wet monster tamed.
Underhood, the minotaur roar of his gears
curses and moves tons. He rockets back to me.

He stops, his head protruding like a turtle
through the square of window. He smiles,
the young stud triumphant, tolerant.
He comes to my rescue, holding
all those hood-hid horses underboot,
but only for a moment. Then he's gone for gas,
the true gallant.

The next week he leaps a rail and rolls his truck
into the muck of the river.
Upturned lies his death chariot, wheels spinning
on their frantic road to nowhere.
Underneath, framed in the square of window
is a trace of face.
No use now my warning that sometimes,
even here, the horses run away.

The New Pump

Two boys who don't spell,
wearing Levis so tight they bend by planning only,
who eat and sleep in baseball caps
hiding their oily curls under lewd sayings,
who can make three wrenches go two ways
while one holds the world still;
two boys who turn cranks and hoist a ton-heavy tank
to swing like an elephant clasped by the talons
of a jubilant pterodactyl,
come in a Dr. Seuss truck
rattling cranes, pulleys, chains
to pull the cancerous innards of the old well
into the light of day
after thirty years of festering.

Two boys who flunked geometry
prod the laws of leverage, of Archimedes' screw,
take off the gauntlet gloves,
and get down to business with bare hands,
forgetting that their father lost a finger
in one slip of a rainy afternoon.

Two boys whose taut muscles bend like eels
to let them lift in dripping mud and rust,
to hoist and coax corroded fittings,
loose rigid joints whose threads are gone
where dank earth and brackish water
sealed them shut as if forever.

Two boys who never wrote a poem
make one in the muddy afternoon.

Walking Her Man

Another couple comes in.
He is holding to her shoulder
like a child playing blind man,
but they are not playing.
She shrugs him off near a chair
which he fingers without lowering his head,
which he uses to anchor his coat,
which he sinks into, neck stiff.
Settled, he opens his eyes.
They are blue. We are surprised.
He closes them again like an empty purse.

She takes out a cellular phone
and talks and smiles.

A sweaty boy brings him a drink without asking.
She talks into the phone, smiling out the window.
He stares straight ahead with his eyes closed
and drinks his drink in silence.

She puts away the phone and looks out the window.
Their stone faces are vacant.

It is like walking the dog, but he's good;
he doesn't spill his drink.

There Went the Bride

We made it through another wedding.
Time now for deep breaths, loosed toes and belts,
perhaps an Alka-Seltzer so that midnight
will not throw us overboard.

It was a lovely wedding. Aren't they all?
Like puppies, are there any ugly ones?
This was one of a series for the bride.
She has a bad habit of marrying her lovers.
Always in white, too; train on the dress,
a hat this time,
and her own daughter for flower girl.

The mothers smile and cry,
but look a little tired.
Putting on weddings can get old fast.
No surprises, just bills, and a different minister
like change of venue for a fair trial.
The same guests in the same
squeaky shoes and tight dresses,
looking carefully at the groom
who must be a lecher underneath the ruffled shirt.
After all, there are no virgins anymore.

Perhaps, we think as the church empties,
perhaps there never were.

Motel in Missoula

Ladies in motel coffee shops
usually wear nice little shirts that go with gray.
They always wear their rings.
They hold their stomachs in when they walk
which gives them the top-heavy look
of hens and opera singers.
They like to think the sensible shoes they wear
are really sensible, not ugly.
They walk, looking straight ahead.

This husband knows the shoes are ugly.
Following behind the lady in the gray skirt,
chin forward against sagging,
eyes on his reflection in the polished window,
he assesses the Hawaiian-print shirt
which Helen gave him for Christmas last year
(or was it the year before?),
the one he wouldn't be caught dead in,
but here he is.

He looks around as he walks the way a child does.
He doesn't like to look at the lady
because she does indeed walk like a hen.
He looks instead at his sensible car, expensive,
but he's made it; he deserves it.
Parked between the yellow lines in front of their room,
it looks pretty classy. He hopes it seems
heavy on the expensive, light on the sensible.
He looks at the concrete walk
where his wife's heels make little clicking sounds.
He is surprised that she leaves no heel prints there.
All that determination and no holes in the sidewalk.

He thinks of other motels long ago,
plastic love palaces with good showers
and white fluffy towels.
He sighs a little at the sensible shoes
and hopes the first cup of coffee will warm his day.

American Legion Convenes
at Big Timber

This armory has no armor.
The sign beside it says, "Saloon Entrance,"
but the saloon is gone.

A beer can rolls across the gravel under its own power,
going nowhere on a last fling.
Hop vines cling to the backside of the defunct saloon,
crazy as clotheslines in photos of Liverpool.
The train rattles through the crossing,
blows a needless warning, but doesn't stop.

The old soldiers arrive wearing blue caps and medals.
Their wives, durable and top-heavy,
wearing those sturdy nurse's shoes
and rayon kerchiefs against the eternal wind,
make their picky way through the gravel,
not ready yet to put on the public smiles.

Chevy pickups and last year's Fords
line up in perfect order.
Inside, before the overdone roast beef,
there are pledges and marches, patriotic songs
sung in creaky falsetto, barely off-key,
while over all floats the great unspoken wish
that for just one day it could be real again,
bullets and all.

Off-Season

Season's over. Slush time now.
People melt like the fickle snow, mush to mud overnight.
No skis anywhere. Snowmobiles sit by dripping walls
like marooned tortoises, silent,
their only virtue above thirty-two degrees.
Potholes where the white ice lay.
Old dogs doze on the asphalt,
soaking up the sun's stingy comfort.

Season's over. We drop the rags of subservience
like hot rocks. Show's over; whatever it is can wait.
Two places open for lunch, using up last week's lettuce.
We show up with people we haven't smiled at
since Thanksgiving. We stamp our mud-filled stompers,
feel the awning's drip slide down our necks,
hitch our jeans, and the place is suddenly a club house.
"I've got chopped ham for omelet, no sliced ham for eggs."
We guess it isn't time for lunch in this part of town.

The old man with real estate
comes in with the wife and the wife's friend,
the skinny one in the wool cap.
She used to be Belle Watling with a husband in the Pentagon.
Now her old Caddie slumps over one tire.
It's lost weight, too.

We sit by two locals who are planning a fish derby for June.
June? When it comes, we'll disappear into our holes like miners,
out of sight, checking, waiting tables,
taking tickets, making other people's beds
or cream pies.

The dogs will move off the asphalt to the dust of the alleys,
worrying occasional cats who dine daintily on careless sparrows.

Now a compact car bulging with fat people pulls up.
Four of them, too large for the Naugahyde chairs,
lean back and order taco salads.
"Are they good?" asks the heavy lady of little faith.
"Yes," hopes the waitress.
Later on we hear as they talk that they have come to foreclose.
One of us didn't make it.
This is how spring comes.
The bottom falls out of the snow, just like the stock market.
Next week, we'll have to eat our own leftovers.

Turncoat

Harry drives home after midnight
regularly now,
down the snow-packed highway
between black trees,
then through the rutted lane
to his dark house
where only the cats are waiting.

Three cats—two strays and an ancient Siamese,
a snob even in these bad times—
all posed in their condescending nonchalance
in perfect trust of his return in predawn,
a time cats love.

She left the old Siamese;
the other two are hobos.
Now in the dark, rubbing the hum against his leg,
the one she left behind joins his ranks,
finding one warm leg as good as another.

It Is Spring–Somewhere

In the off-season these woods assume a smugness,
claiming encroachments on the town,
whispering of its temporariness in their midst,
sighing, dripping resentments,
sending out feelers of return.

In the dark, a thousand eyes glimmer contempt
at the islands of orange neon:
BAR OPEN and HAPPY HOUR.
The puddles freeze over at sunset;
the motel parking places are pockmarks in the mud.

Inside, brave lights glow enough to show us the regulars:
the bartender with his boot upon the chair;
the cook, lonely from the useless kitchen,
come to listen in on last week's jokes;
the local leader whose wife is home hacking away at death
while he urges oblivion in the corner seat,
all made cozy by the poker machine
perking and bubbling in its corner,
leading a life of its own.

This is life, camaraderie in the midst of wilderness,
warmth against the creeping woods,
a holding-off of nightmare and of guilt.
"Don't mention Rosie's eye," the cook whispers
as the waitress, picking up the tip from the only customer,
weeps quietly through her blackened orb.

Cattle Drive up the Madison

Cars and campers wait, second-class spectators
while the show moves through.
Kids watch, agog. This is no Disneyland.
Steers, dogs, cows, calves,
cowboys, real ones with snarling teeth,
sitting horses, moving critters like syrup,
yard by yard.

Cattle, brown eyes bulging,
feet klaketty on the highway,
tails held high to insult us with dung,
stupid beyond belief, but lovely
in the necessity to stay together,
programmed to be in bunches,
move ten miles sideways to gain one;
steer stands in silhouette across both lanes,
posing for Charlie Russell.

That little Appaloosa to the left
moves up and down the borrow pit,
stepping high, a circus pony
turning on a dime by the twist of a hand,
remembering painted riders bareback
through bison herds.

The spotted dog, one eye blue, one eye brown,
plays point counterpoint, feinting,
twisting, inexhaustible.

Some car from Kentucky honks. Bad form.
The patterns waver.
Two pups doze on the warm asphalt.
And not a single cowboy sings about Laredo.

High Places

Henry, no longer young, took to the summit path
in street shoes, altitude be damned.
Henry, who worked for God in the outer office,
suspected they were vacationing together,
picnicking near this path.
It was not the sort of place one expects
to run into the boss, but Henry's
has a habit of being in unusual environs.

The path, as advertised, led to a small rise
poking a hole into the blue sky,
a bump of rocks and bushes
out of which ran two small streams of water.

A small sign said

> *Continental Divide*
> *Waters to the left flow to the Pacific Ocean*
> *Waters to the right flow to the Atlantic Ocean*

The tiny rivulets, small as the waters
of Henry's garden hose at home,
gurgled around the rock dividing them.

Henry, never before having felt the urge
to move mountains, bent and with his own two hands
dammed up the Atlantic,
diverting the mini-river into the Pacific.
At once the Atlantic dried up, its sand bottom
shrinking in this sudden aridity.

112

"I have changed the course of mighty rivers.
I have the powers of the seas in my two hands."
He glowed at the immensity of his achievement
until his back began to ache,
and he conceded that omnipotence can be tiring.
Besides, wasn't it a trifle boring holding the seas at bay?
Had not even Atlas longed for a change of job description
after certain muscles near the spinal axis tired?

Sighing, Henry stood up, feeling the relief
of blood and breath renewed.
As he watched, the Atlantic dutifully took up its course
and gurgled again in its eastern bed.
Henry washed the sand from his holy hands,
brushed the leaves from his celestial trousers
and walked back to his waiting car,
tendering a smile upward
as he listened to the distant roar of two mighty oceans
girding the earth at his whim.

At the Charles M. Russell Gallery

Great Falls, Montana

This gallery is polite, like a mortuary.
We whisper as in hospital corridors.

The paintings are good; the sculptures are better.
They are small and delicate
as if he were about to run out of materials.
They gather no dust now under glass.
People think of them as sacred objects,
but he gave them away for drinks and smokes.

"Some are better than me, some worse,"
he said. "At least, I do what I like."
He liked wolves.

The gallery tries to hold him together.
The illuminated letters are neatly framed and hung,
stamped envelopes included.
All the way along the corridors
under the diffused lighting,
we marvel that those people had sense enough
to save his stuff. How did they know?

Even a letter from Leonardo
probably wouldn't make it
through the 4.3 U-Haul moves
they say we'll all make
during our 1.0 lifetimes.

Message from a Deserted Cabin

The old man left with no intention of dying.
He would be back to do surgery on the front step,
to replace the screen on the dog pen,
straighten the chimney, buck up the woodpile,
repair the cat door.
The wren house is on its side in the grass.
No wrens this year, either.

The beer can under the old wagon
isn't the old man's fault.
His boat, upside down by the back door
like a yellow tortoise, leaks, even here.

Things are askew about the house,
shutters warp to rakish angles,
chinking loosens, returning to earth.
Tired boards creak, losing the desire to be a house,
wanting instead to retire as a marmot apartment—
at least until the next quake.

The marmots are inside again, nesting in the bathtub.
There are holes, subways they watched him plug up
with wire while they sharpened their incisors.
Their relatives watch now
from a neighbor's neat woodpile.

Perhaps he is sitting atop the woodpile, too,
waiting for me and my disapproval to leave,
waiting to chuckle to the marmots to get on with it,
to chew up his boat as well,
for he will fish now without need of it.

About the Author

A native of Utah, Jan Dunbar earned a degree from UCLA, married a fly-fisher, and eventually moved with him to West Yellowstone, Montana. There she obtained a master's degree in English at Montana State University, taught for over thirty years, and watched with some amazement as her two children grew up. She began writing poetry no more than a dozen years ago. Since then she has won contests sponsored by the Montana Institute of the Arts, the Pacific Northwest Writers, and the Washington Poets Association and has been published by such magazines as *Yokoi*, *Plainswoman*, and *Gray's Sporting Journal*. Her work has also appeared in several anthologies, including *Aurora* and *Montana Sketchbook*. *The Overlay of Random and Order* is her first book of poetry.